POEMS 2020

POEMS 2020

Goutam Jena

Translated by
Himanshu Parida

BLACK EAGLE BOOKS
Dublin, USA | Bhubaneswar, India

BLACK EAGLE BOOKS

USA address:
7464 Wisdom Lane
Dublin, OH 43016

India address:
E/312, Trident Galaxy, Kalinga Nagar,
Bhubaneswar-751003, Odisha, India

E-mail: info@blackeaglebooks.org
Website: www.blackeaglebooks.org

First International Edition Published by
BLACK EAGLE BOOKS, 2025

POEMS 2020
by **Goutam Jena**
Chahata, Dharmasala, Jajpur- 755008
Odisha, India, Cell-9237481405
Email: jena.goutam1959@gmail.com

Translated by **Himanshu Parida**

Original Copyright © Goutam Jena
Translation Copyright © Himanshu Parida

All rights reserved. No part of this publication may be reproduced, stored in a retrieval system, or transmitted, in any form or by any means, electronic, mechanical, photocopying, recording or otherwise without the prior permission of the publisher.

Cover & Interior Design: Ezy's Publication

ISBN- 978-1-64560-645-1 (Paperback)

Printed in the United States of America

For those departed souls
who died of pandemic Corona.
– poet

Foreword

Poem as a literary form has the ability to touch everything across the world, may it be the wide expanse of vast land, mountains, water bodies, deserts, gorges, space and sea everywhere. Anything lying anywhere, even anything not appearing or existing but imagined can make a poem. Poem does not depend on validation as a truth in the traditional belief. It does not restrict the areas which are visible and can also be perceived by any of our sense organs. Secondly poetry creates magic in words by associating not only what it means literally or lexically but also contextually and referentially.

Goutam Jena as a poet of repute has not only mastered the art of word use but also has the capability to touch all the aspects of life visible and not visible but coming under the area of awareness of the poet. The poem collection which is named 'Poems 2020' has strictly not restricted its realm of poetic world in the short period of 2020 which basically disturbed the poetic mind of poet Goutam Jena with the awe stricken by pandemic, Corona, forcing him to compose altogether different aspects of his encountering Corona.

It is in fact a great pleasure for me to translate my friend Goutam Jena's poems which I have read for a considerable long period in different literary magazines of Odisha of repute. The poet has touched not only the woes faced by thousands of people suffering from corona and many with them who are affected by the dreaded disease either living every day with the terror of imminent death but also covered the experiences and feelings of many, who as family members and near and dears have to bear the pain of nursing people to get them out from the clutches of Corona. Goutam Jena's specialty in his poetic treatment of the theme is that he never philosophises what he observes. He simply puts his words matching with the intensity of feeling the characters and situations have generated in him. The basic poetic treatment of a topic by Goutam Jena is that he holds the topic as he sees it or visualizes it. Accordingly, to match the intensity of feeling he presents the subject in poetry with the wonder expressed by a pure soul.

The collection has 42 poems on different topics and subjects. The book starts with the address of the poet to his own self and gets the reader ready for giving the readers as if a preparatory lesson for experiencing his poetry in their own life. Many of the poems of Goutam Jena are more of a confessional statement. Sometime his excess of obsession with certain topics makes him biased and full of eulogy.

But he has a tremendous skill of resolution in the poem comprising different views. The poet's declaration of his personality is in the following words in his poem; 'To Me'

> "I have never been in advertisements.
> Thrown into the dustbin
> I wait for someone to pick me up
> Considering me as a valuable
> Then I am precious.
> If I am thrown as a piece of glass
> I lie as a piece of glass only.
> If you mix up diamond with pieces of glass
> Who has the skill to separate it off!
> Only a perfect eye can find the difference
> That it is of worth."

The above statement speaks of what the poet is. The poet wants to create a different world of his own where his words shall be his own. The topics chosen by the poet, e.g. Lockdown, In search of Happiness, India that is India, Love for Country, Traitor etc are definitely are from a wide canvas which does not restrict the poems to a specific time period. Rather for the poet the poetic world is an extraction of events from the huge field of time just to understand the reason behind a great chain of events.

Besides holding his specific and unique view on the subjects in his poems poet Goutam Jena believes in putting suitable words to express his most private emotions and feelings. For poet Goutam Jena his poems are the medium in the quest of the ultimate truth. Also for him words alone do not suffice for discovering the truth of life. Its feelings aligned with words which are in a permanent journey for finding the ultimate truth of life to get the real taste of life lived on this earth.

Hopefully Goutam Jena's poem translated in English shall definitely catch the attention of a wide readership across India cutting across many languages who are connected with one another by the strong bond of English language. I wish all the best to the poet and also to this work of art.

Date- 18/09/2024 **Himanshu Parida**
Cuttack

Contents

To Me	13
Lockdown-1	15
Lockdown-2	17
Lockdown-3	19
Lockdown-4	21
This time I am prepared to accept you	22
In Search of Happiness	24
Bad Times	26
The Life encountered afresh	28
On the Western Horizon	30
Modi	32
India that is India-1	36
India that is India-2	37
India that is India-3	38
A Sad Tale	40
Accident	43
Dance	45
I want to sing a song	47
Destiny	49

A mourning for an indifferent time	51
Invoking Peace	53
Inconsolable	56
Retirement	58
Silence	60
Under the Spell of the Earth	62
Love for my Country	64
The Traitor	66
The school is over	68
What you have undergone	70
An Unknown Thrill	72
A Journey	74
The Bird	76
Fullstop	78
To Love	80
Reverberations	82
Completeness	85
A Kiss	87
Deceit	89
Lost Childhood	91
How many more days	93
The Last word: Hope	96

To Me

I have never been in advertisements.
Thrown into the dustbin
I wait for someone to pick me up
Considering me as a valuable
Then I am precious.
If I am thrown as a piece of glass
I lie as a piece of glass only.
If you mix up diamond with pieces of glass
Who has the skill to separate it off!
Only a perfect eye can find the difference
That it is of worth.
Everywhere you have a problem
To search the true diamond among the glass pieces
Although you may be late
But to grade grains of paddy from chaff
May be under our control.
I salute the person who has spent
All his life in search a grain of paddy and a diamond.

I am not among awardees
Not even applauded in praise
I am not in any group, divisions
I am all alone
Unique.
Still if someone chooses me as his company
And makes me his dearest of dears!!
All these men are gods
And these gods form the foundations of my thoughts.
The abstract dreams of my unconscious
I offer my prayers to those dreams.
From earth to ether
Lying in between all known and unknown
Fetched and unfetched
Pleasures enjoyed and abstentions
In the darkness of illusions
He who takes charge of the Truth hidden
To decipher and identify
All his efforts and expectations
Become a part of the process of a labyrinth;
A mystery unsolved
And as an unwanted identity
Who is left as such
I offer my respect to that Man.

Lockdown-1

This time man is
In a posture of surrender.
For long sixty years
It's a history, a pathetic tale of a
Life in peril
Which is pulverizing even a chest made of stone.
The dread of corona has spread across the World
Every moment there is a doubt on my chance of survival
A thick screen of fog
Dense darkness
Covers the surface of earth with melancholy.

In a world of addition and deletion
Who can say
Who stays where
And is where from ?
Is it so that everything is at your option?
It's only that you boast.

The man is no other than
Who is summoned by death
With whispers …come, come on.
Till you are alive ask from the earth
All the joy in its treasure.
But everything changes.
All our desires and thoughts
Crossing the limit of wish and reluctance
undergo for a change.
Today who is thought as yours
The next day he is your enemy
And the enemy of today is the most dear
Tomorrow.

Who would be capable of giving so much of joy
Other than this earth!
At God's will tomorrow everything would be different
The new sun will touch the earth
And lead us to a new path for a living.

Lockdown-2

Whatever is going on till today,
What is the benefit of searching those?
What is the use of remembering those??

Someone is calling me from my front
Leading me holding my hand
Shows me the rising sun
And the flowers bloomed.

To be lost picking up the flowers fallen off
What is the benefit of shedding tears
 Emotionally?
Shall the dreams ever return?
Can the joyful years spent as age
Shall ever come back?

We have to go on living
Even losing everything
Again, painting with colours our inside

We have to celebrate.
Whatever happiness
We can bring back from memory
Let us store it for a lifetime.

How to live
that secret would be revealed by Time
Still, someone steals that loneliness
And pats me to sleep whole night
With promises of dreams to live
Ages together.

Lockdown-3

Yes,
The morning where it would arrive
We shall search there another World.
We would leave behind
On hundreds of corpses
A putrefying earth
And the darkness breaking our chest
Into multiple pieces.
With half a life and half death
We have spent our days
Still never did time leave me unattended
And intoxicated.
Everywhere there the flow of honey
From grey fields
And from dry and desolate sky
The chirping of birds.

Happiness multiplies when distributed
And sorrow dies within

Then why should I blame the time
Why should I think of settling the score?
All my mistakes are nothing but
Pieces of my moment's thirst.

One day we have to depart
Alone,
If my mood breaks down
The night full of dreams may end in daybreak.
Still, I have to reach the end of this road
I have to go.

Lockdown-4

For a long time, I had a desire
That I should be in jail
Can I not be jailed?
Whatever way I sought
Nothing could satisfy me.
If I would beat someone
People will brand me as a goon
If I would tease somebody
People will tell me a loafer
All these which came to mind
Could not give me a way out.

As usual I got retired from service
Still, I could not get a chance to fulfil my desire
Truly speaking this was my last chance
All over the state lockdown is imposed
If you would come out
Under Section 270
At least two years of jail.
Yes now a days jail is more secure than home!
Should I miss the chance?
Give me if you can the appropriate advice
Still I am waiting.

This time I am prepared to accept you

Now the earth is unstable
Maybe I have to say goodbye
To this world.

Every moment the dread of death
Surrounds me from every side
With eyes turned red with blood
Invites me
Calls me, indicates me.

I do not have any regret
Each time death exalted with arrogance
Breaking asunder with its proud presence
Call me, indicate me by hand.

Now I have a feeling that
Everything happened wrong
Now where to go!

Everywhere it is disjointed and non-appended.
A helplessness and melancholy
Has overpowered the world
And had confined it in quarantine to rest and recuperate.

I am coming back crossing the boundary of
A prohibited region
My feet, my hands and my mouth
Are in action as it is
Then what is there to be afraid of?

I could hear someone singing at a far-off place
Absorbed in music he has an overwhelming urge
To embrace the whole world.
There is no reason to fear
Now I am prepared to claim as my own
The whole sky, earth
The whole lot of exploited men
and all the sorrows of the world.
I shall make a new earth.

In Search of Happiness

It is surprising that
 From the deep darkness
Again like a luminous light
A soul comes out.
From the space to the earth
Everywhere myriad flowers
in different colours covered
Overwhelmed by an intimate embracing
Forget the catastrophe of the pandemic
And the apprehensions and regrets.

Till today no such untoward incident has taken place
Whatever changes those happened
In our day to day life, habits and thinking
are as usual.
The desire to complete a half-built earth
Remains always incomplete.
Let us forget this bad time

Let us not wear the mask
Let us forget to keep social distance.
Let smile sprout in our lips
Let us hold one another in deep embrace
And build a new World.

History is an unwanted sheet of paper
It devours the civilization like a python
And teaches us lie
It plays with our thinking and emotion.
Nothing to surprise
We shall defeat this virus
In our search for happiness.

Bad Times

We are born during a time
At the crossroads of a good time
And a bad time.
So we have to face the consequences
And we have to fight against all the impending dangers.

We have to face the adversity
And we have to enjoy every bit of life
With pomp and royalty.

At this time everything
Unbound wealth, name and fame
Awards have no meaning.
All the time we probe into our life in a dark tunnel.

In the deep sea on a small boat
We are closing in to death.
Still, we have to gather courage

And determined with patience
And learn the art of living.

Now the whole world is in isolation
And quiet
The same sky, the same sun
The same moon and as usual those stars
But in the funeral procession of so many dead bodies
Flowers corrugate and wither away
Myriad wishes and probabilities
Fall flat on earth.

Oh Men!
Now with folded hands
Beg excuses
Lock from inside all the envy and anger.
Let this twenty first century be
Of living a Life and charity.

The Life encountered afresh

Now I am going to tell you about a virus
Which bestrides on my shoulder at every day break
And terrifies me.
Oh!
Why am I so gripped with fear!
Death is like a wild animal
Striding towards me and scaring me with its horns.
Every moment,
In spite of this I face him bravely.

We may not be there
But after us someone definitely
Put this earth in order
Adorning with moon and garlands of stars.

Let us be grateful to
Trees and overgrowths of foliage,
Let us be grateful to the air and to the whole creation.
In such a life imprisoned with stagnation
They are feeling the elixir of life
And enthusiasm of life to live.

The roads now are slippery
How long we would be hiding in this shell
Sluggishly like a snail ?
I can see the waterfall of Ghagara
And the hot water spring of Atri
As well as Konark, Kapilas,
Saptashajya and so on…..
I can hear the sound of birds chirping
If not from far off Chilika but from Anshupa.
Everywhere with a boisterous cheer
Life goes on
Then why inside me an unknown fear goes on lamenting?

Is there a heaven somewhere?
No,
This time you please touch me
How long I shall bear the pain of
Not getting your touch?
Here everything will be over
Including all pondering, speaking out, writing and obtaining.
Then what I shall do with heavenly bliss.

We both are strangers until today
Let us be well known to each other
Let us be most dear to each other.
Years together, months long, days passing on
We shall not waste our time in searching each other
In a moment we shall discard the old time
And shall meet a life renewed.

On the Western Horizon

In the glow of the sun at the western horizon
The entire world got dazzled.
From the sky gradually appeared
A bunch of white moustaches in a pale face
under the round spectacles
and a line of golden smile there.

There was already daybreak
People in groups with tricolours in hand
Were resounding the whole earth
With chanting of 'Janagana mana'.

The trees and shrubs, rivers and rivulets,
hills and mountains were in extreme rejoice
They have been free
Erasing the taint of bondage from their forehead
They are now addressing the birds
To fill them with the song of delight
And animate with life a dead-like stagnant life.

The whole world has seen
How in the sword of such a valiant warrior
There was not even a drop of blood
But the country became free.
Nonviolence is such a sword
At the sight of which even a dreadful tiger
Bends his head in respect and disperse
With a posture of surrender.

Under the spread of the arms of a short statured man
A goddess like auspicious image is drawn
From the tunes of Ramdhun
The call for making of India of future comes out.
Ah!
That man has become a sea of memory
And built a high rising tower of grand freedom
In our soul.

Modi

A great opportunity was available
To read selected books
Sitting whole day
And write poetry and criticism.

Twenty-four hours of lockdown
Was flashing
The unruly men's struggle to live.
Everywhere amidst a continuous struggle
Each human being was scrambling for a puff of breath.

Streets are desolate and lonely
On the slippery sun
Lanes and by-lanes including trees
Are helplessly balancing.
Temples and mosques are locked
Fairs and celebrations are suspended indefinitely.
Among all these close downs
Human beings have been counting
Every moment of their lifetime.

Just see!
Someone is continuously walking forward
Awake all along
Without feeling hunger.
Unshaven melancholic face full of beard
Till now the hymn of owning up
Has not been extinguished.

From the pocket of trouser
Unending traces of dreams
Get released as in an explosion.
The whole of the country
India gets spell bound.

He has been cleaning
the hanging gossamers and dirts
filling up the pits and potholes
has been mending the torn clothes.
He has been walking down a long way
In ups and downs
Till he touches the horizon
Until he touches people's hearts.

Bagchi

From one mirror
Like a dazzling noon getting reflected
The top was visible.
How can there be so much of expectations
And so much of excitements
From one picture unknown and unheard of
Was multiplying our unquenched thirst!

The picture which was drawn
In our soul was uniquely artistic
Moreover, we can say,
In this side there was unending stretches of water
On the other side there was licking of flames of fire
Which endeavors to gorge and digest
In between Bagchi
Appears in a pose of fine balance.

What is to us if the trees are in bloom
And full of flowers
the sky gets full of stars
but if a sweet fragrance spreads
and the moon appears in the sky
Automatically our heart leaps with joy
And all the fears, apprehensions and worries
Are pushed away.

My look looks like an open story book,
The reader reads leisurely whenever he wants.
He sees two calm eyes appearing on the cover page,
The sweet lips
And irrespective of these
The patience of the unending time
Glittering on his uncovered face.

(Dedicated to the great personality Subrat Bagchi)

India that is India-1

Within a night the map of a country may change
Building fresh ridges and boundaries
A new geographical region is made.
Again, a new history is written.

As if a new World
A new belief system
Got attached in the tradition of Bharat
And in its heritage.

It seems as if some men newly formed
Would fly like free birds in the sky
With delight and excitement.

Yes, this was to happen since a long time
What has now happened.
The lost souls have come back to
Their own body.
The forgotten melodies are reverberating
Inside us.
Soon after a miraculous sunrise touched the earth
The earth turned to heaven.
A pinch of dust as soon as one holds
It smelt like Bharat and Bharat.

India that is India-2

When I listen to the victory cries
As if in me a rare thrill is created.
In me automatically such a map is drawn
That I hum a song in its praise.

In me I have an apprehension
as much as I feel a delight.
As much as I turn into a hard stone with cruelty.
To give security to a handful of soil
I to that extent I convert into the flowing melody of a rivulet
Just to offer my unbound affection.

What connection do I have with this soil?
What for some times a terrorist in me
Becomes a cruel self of me
Against the executioners of this soil's life source
I do not what is there in this soil
For which before me it appears
As if Bharat.

India that is India-3

At last, I got you
But in the process, I was lost in the ages of dreams
When I was lost, I did not know even
The plight of loss.

You were an inner page of the tattered book of history
You were a torn map cut with a sharp knife.
The beauty of your body was pale
Like the eclipsed moon
Looked at me with a desolate gaze
With a desire to adopt me.

This time we shall march ahead,
Far from this place
Where only dreams be
And beyond the reach of everyone.
 A trace of sorrow even cannot
Touch our shadows.
Let's go there, both of us.

Now the sky would be full of colours
In the soil everywhere the tune of a fluteplayer's music
Shall be permeating.
On the other side
with the evening drooping on the earth
With a pathetic tune
There would be the shadow of a wet sun.
My two eyes would be by this time
Measuring our intimate relationship of years together.
From the freezing cold womb
One touch of a warm hand
Would be spreading to my whole entity.
A magical touch again shall
Make me frenzied
Telling me Bharat my dear Bharat.

A Sad Tale

Had anyone told regarding this
Little sad tale?
From where the words shall be
Arranged in order
And from where the introduction of
Sorrow shall start
And from where the sad tale would end
Has it to anybody's knowledge?

Its sorrowful when you inhale
And in your long breath .
Sorrow comes with words
As well as with silence.
There is sorrow in earth
And, in the sky.

In five senses sorrow felt
And in our five natures
And in five elements
You find sorrow inherent.

Sometimes I have doubt on the
Ability of words
My relationship, dreams and realizations
Come to me in what colours,
In what beats it appear,
In what rhyme scheme it is composed,
And in which circumference it revolves,
I do not know.
In what caption it is identified
I do not know.

At times these words are boundless
Like the space
And some other time who can explain
How it is intelligible like life and soul
Cannot be imagined
As this is half visible and half invisible.
I cannot recognize
Cannot even understand
It just appears before my eyes
And sometimes not present
Both come to my memory and soon forgotten
Become clear and then disappear.

Still, I am in search of this
Strides before me straight
Looking back, it gestures me
But in my eyes the whole earth is glowing
And I am possessed by hundreds of mountain peaks.

Yes, I fly like a lonely bird
And like a torn kite
Directionless
Pushing aside the dense fog
To tell my tale of woe.

Accident

Every accident has a history
It might be known to someone
Or might be altogether unknown
Automatically a cobweb by a spider is created
And like some flies unnecessary thing get caught.
When an analysis is made, they become the cause.

Yes, an accident is not only an accident.
Its not only a portion of history
With it many people's destiny get entangled.
With that time period bad times all
Sins and good deeds
And result of a deeds.

Bravo! In the giant canvas of a whole life spent
Like a kite fallen from the sky
Watching an aimless life
The dreams, possibilities and trust
Disappear.

The maelstrom of faith inside my chest
which has met with an accident
Is no less than a tornado
Affinity bursts and disappears like a water bubble.

From birth till death
Every day, every moment gets dissected
Whether it is the auspicious time of conjugal relationship
I do not know whether it is under the malefic spell of Rahu
Or due to influence of Saturn in my fate
My period of prosperity eludes me
And my detractors pull me down.
In a moment all my success meets with an accident
And as if half dead for a long time.

An accident is an accident
To ponder over it
Whether it's God's will
Or someone's conspiracy
Is useless.
All these one has to accept
Frequently like Arjuna with helplessness.
And one must surrender
Before the invisible power
Without diffidence.

Dance

I made such a sky
Where there was also a moon and number of stars
And millions of earths.
Among those I was in one earth.

In this earth
One side is bright
And the other side is dark
In one side there is embrace
And at the other side is exile.
At times the human blood
Changes altogether.

I do not know, who clipps
The wings of love from the birds
And leave them paralysed?
Still the marks appearing like horizon
Shifts like my dreams
In an eternal time.
Every moment every incident
Makes me spell bound.

Someone appearing like God
Instructs me to dance
And makes me forgetful
And lost in myself
And soon after it leads me holding my hands
To a vociferous clamour.

It seems as if all are dancing
Not being conscious of what they do
The water, wind, trees
And even the mountains and the sea
All dance in a frenzy.

At last, when I open my eyes
I find myself all alone
Fighting against my own existence.
Almost everybody has deserted me
No one with me neither a near dear nor
Any relation.
In the meantime, I put my body to a new cage
Inside me
Completely Unaware of this.

I want to sing a song

I want to sing a song
A song in an exalted state
A song that makes me lose myself.

I want to sing such a song
In which years after years shall disappear
Putting aside greed, ambition and dreams.

To confine my forgetfulness
There is no codes and prison.
To erase dreams
You would not get support from woes,
And someone's impartial thoughts.
Just with closed eyes
Loiter wherever you wish
You shall see
Whatever you wish you would get that,
I want to sing such a song.

Has anyone lived without loving something!
He may be a bird freed
Or may be free breath exhaled
This handful of breath gets ventilated
In the strong cage of my love
Which is in a state of dream perennially,
With it I shall travel in the whole sky flapping my wings.
I want to sing such a song.

When you sing
Is it necessary to
Search the meaning?
Meaning will automatically appear
Like dreams
And overpower your whole body, mind and thoughts
Even your emotion and your journey
Without destination.
Where there would be happiness in bounty
The morning of delight which
When your eyes cannot gauze
And dazzling all the time.
I want to sing such a song.

Now why should I be afraid of dark nights?
He would come and get lost in the broad daylight.
All around all our dreams shall be flaring up with light
All those wishes to get free
Shall appear as invisible bodies.
I want to sing such a song.

Destiny

Everywhere you would find frustration
Sitting quietly weeping incessantly.
Time slips from the fist
Relations slips away from the surroundings.
Time is for facing it upfront
Shedding tears
Losing a remix of symphony.

This is such a cruel earth
Which takes away
Our emotions and memories.
Only it gives us loneliness and pain
A heartful of sorrow and desperation.
Exactly at that time
People think of God
And pray helplessly
Asking for security.

At that time flowers lose their
Fragrance
All the rivers change their course
The sea gets dried up
And lie desperately.
Still efforts are made
to see the next morning
out of all unsuccessful trials
as the time is not favourable.

Every morning comes like this
Most aspired for
Among all the apprehensions and doubts
A moonlit night is promised
Every time in our cupped palms to offer.
It is like every time we have to turn over
The calendar.
Can anybody guarantee
That from the lines of our palm
The future would come out clear
And in our cursed fate the reddish bright sun
Shall rise in the morning break !!

A mourning for an indifferent time

Exactly one confused state
Disturbs me all the time.
The reason of it is not known
But it makes all opportune moments
In my reach messy.
I don't know from when
I have developed enmity with time,
For which all my exalted times passed
Repel the upcoming moments.
My body and I are quite separate
Placed apart at a million-distance length
And I swim in a chasm away from the end.
I forget myself
Forget my nears and dears around me
I do not know, who makes me so forgetful
Everywhere I face a desolate cosmic space,
A body full of sweats and tears
And a pathetic moaning of
A helpless body.

I am there
My body is also there
There lies my wish
The resigned state of my entire entity.
Still, someone questions me
Again and again
At least this time I should
Open completely all the covers
Of pretensions
To recognise myself.
And get immersed there
To search for what is inside me in every life.

Invoking Peace

I watch; how everyday
The dazzling white bodies of the days
Entering deep darkness.
This darkness is strange and unknown
Like an unsatisfied soul
Overpower me with an unending hunger.

How long
For how many years
This lockdown shall continue
With the shutdown paralysing
The speaking powers
Being afraid of losing our identity
Man meets death again and again.

This time
Every bodily being raise their hands
In submission
And screech in agony
Which elongates from the graveyard
Up to Salvation
Continuously for long

How many times
We grieve from inside
And grope for many things
Including ourselves.
Whatever we fetch
Are all unwanted and unexpected
Whatever are not available
Rot in a sense of scarcity.

All the opposite of thoughtfulness
Are not necessarily thoughtlessness
Which all on a sudden scratch and
Dig out all satisfactions.

Who is there to drag me
With an invisible rope
Throws my soul
In between destiny and deserved.

This time I must come back
Carrying the loads of agony out of
That which I did not get.
Within a moment
The whole sea I shall drink
With my handful
And satiate my thirst
I shall smear your whole body with
Incense, sandal wood and invoke you with an earthen lamp.
Oh, my compassionate deity
Give me peace
Peace! Peace!! Peace!!!

Inconsolable

A firepot of discontentment burns
Inside my chest
And I am not able to console myself.

This fire burns my whole body
After burning the wildly grown unruly weeds
Inside me.
Still a man prepares to die
Than to be a coward.

A man swims in the unfathomable depth of water
to reach a lotus
which drifts gradually.

Inhaling the flower offered by an old flower woman
My desperation and unintelligibility
transform into an innocence like that of a lamb.

Oh!
I feel as if all along I have been a stranger to myself.
The visions I see
The topics coming to my mind
The emotion I feel
The memories I have long back left behind
All as if are gradually moving away from me.

My mind appears more laden black
Than the sky full of black clouds
My thoughts are as if loads
More than the weights posed by the hills and mountains,
Asif everything is in helter-skelter
And run away from me.

In my front only
I observe the never-before blending in unison
Of sound and words
With which the morning breaks.

Almost the embrace of heaven and earth
Overwhelms me with an intimate feeling.

I am blinded and grope
To identify my corpse from the
Graveyard of the past
To carry it with a desperate cry.

Retirement

I no longer require watching
The clock
No more, I need to know the date.

Leaving aside
The hot midday
Evening and night
What is there for me in time!
What is for me from those days
Numbered in a week!!

In so many days in a week
How evening comes
And how day breaks
I had not thought of those.
The changing date in a calendar
Also appear useless sometimes.

When do I look for some rest
Leisure
To arrange my self
From all my thoughts and all my engagements!

Is there any routine
Any timetable!
Its only to console the agitated mind
And retirement means for me
Rest from the jobs getting lost.

I have come back to you again.
This soil, water, air
Dreams, rivers
Dense forest, fields,
The calls of the mountains
All these have brought me back.

Silence

In the fading lights of the twilight
About to arrive
I can feel
The heat of the fire
Coming to me slowly all by itself.
This time somehow an intimate spell of hypnosis
Was drawing us to each other.

The warmth of that fire already forgotten
Has already overpowered my thought
with a renewed shape.
A fireball shown to the earth
Was not only a wonder
But it was appearing like a difficult formula
Of a mathematical calculation.

Neither I can leave the ground
Nor I can overlook the stretched hand of the sky
Never seen before !
But the song sung by the sky
Draw me to another morning
Wading through the crowding
Of planets and satellites.

Till now I am not able to
Recognise the entity
Who calls me from my inside
To come down and see
How in the first sight of someone
Glowing with a bright light
Can make me so near and dear.

I wonder; who is he?
Who does not understand the magic of seasons
Who even does not know how a season attracts
He does know how he himself casts a spell on others
And he does not decipher the language of heart.
Who is he??
Who is he??

No!
This does not have an answer.
Although some one knows about this
Why does he ask of it at all !
This question again and again
Come back to me in the shape of echoes.

At last, this fire catches in the body
Till it burns and turn into ashes
And all the questions mingle with earth
Turning into dust.

Under the Spell of the Earth

Dreams are broken into pieces
And I must fix them again
To pass the whole night.

This night
Is not the whole night.
But millions of nights
Pounce upon me and capture me
Like an unquenched spirit.

In the process of waiting for long years
My eyes turn into ant hills.
A feeble voice oozes out of it
Which neither is audible
Nor recognized
Everywhere somehow a helplessness
Out of sense of strange feelings
Overpowers me
And agitates me for a long time.

No!
Earth only shows you dream
And delights
Teaches you to love
And gives you separation also.
The more it makes you its own
Likewise, it torments you
Treating you as someone unknown.
It gives you happiness
And also kills you with woes.

This separation
These broken dreams
The night of tormentations is not over
The dreaming of people is not yet over.
In the intimacy of a handful of soil
To the extent one gets engrossed
He forgets everything to be lost in that
Loss
Lost and lost completely.

Love for my Country

As I have come here
One day I have to leave
May it be today or tomorrow.
Would I have bothered
Had it been that
Things happened as I had wished.
For that only I surrendered everything
To the earth
What I had stored
And what was my due.

I did not come to you
To ask for anything
Whatever you had given me
I returned those
Rather I gave you more
My affection and attachment
For my future generation
Along with that my valour, grit and patriotism.

Till I was on this earth
My life was only transactions of give and take.
In between friendship and enmity
Drawing lines between own and others.
Once we leave this earth
Tell me, would we be able to meet again!!

Look, in front of us roads have dispersed
To different directions
Whichever way you would go
Whichever song you would sing
whichever language you do speak
Again, we would meet
At last, in a destined place definitely.

Whether love or hate
For this time
It is a peculiar question.
No one may listen to it or not
But not for today only
We must safely store the earth
For another thousand years.

Life is not only a boat without destination
To drift in the endless sea
It is not even a battle ground
Which would scratch and extract from us
All the tears and agony.
To mingle with the earth and be one with it
Is a grand meditation
The earth only can give
A feeling of exaltation eternally.

The Traitor

When the whole day is gradually over
The black curtain of the evening spreads
From the earth to the sky.
Exactly at that time
Thousands of lamps get lit
Inside me
Which lights up my soul
And my whole consciousness.
So many days and so much brightness
Where these ultimately disappear silently
I do not know !
Its only darkness and darkness
Which cannot stop the journey.
Inside me amidst a garland of lights
I can see something so dear to me
Crystal clear.

This earth gives life and takes it away also
As it delights it also burns with melancholy.
It may dazzle in myriad colours
Or might be burning with a colourless hue
But everywhere the song of living
Is to be sung.

Everywhere this living
Paints every day and every night
Either with song of happiness
Or with the song of tears.
And what happens in the meanwhile
To the nights!
It follows me like a traitor
And at the opportune moment
Puts a load of melancholy on my head
And laughs at my agony.
Oh! I only pity these nights.

How miserable are these nights!
Within no time disappear
When faced with a firm belief.
At last, they surrender
And bow before that all the time.

The school is over

The school bell has rung
Now gradually evening would come
And night would fall
And the men treading on untrodden ways
Shall be fast asleep quietly.

Sleep comes on its own
As such there are no determinations
And commitments to return.
Still if someone would return
For him there might be another morning
I case he does not return
He would find the desolate cry of a bad harvest.

When the bell rings to tell; the school is over
The baby birds wait for their mother
Returning to the nest.

The flooded river in rainy days
Flow backward
It spells a magical moment
On every feeling nerve
Overpowered by a painful obsession.
This is such a thrilling moment
Where one fills in his fist the whole sky
And affects from earth to sky
In a spell of dream.

Everywhere
With the piles of dreams
An intimate magic is created,
Which in the clutches of hugs tightly
Many more births of mine.

I get lost inside me
And turn into a indifferent word
A feeble sound
Inside a speck of dust
With delight and happiness completely.

What you have undergone

Inside my body the clock
Which ticks
Can that indicate me
How long I have to wait on this earth!

We all know, as long as this clock works
Till that time everything is fine with us
We look healthy and hearty
Inside us the dreams design
Beautiful sky studded with moon and stars
And in our mind a sea full with innumerable tides
Appear.

The clock runs incessantly
Validating all the errors and miscalculations.
Within a moment all my faith and determination
Give way like a bubble in water.

All my feeling of my own crumble
And turn into an apparition.
Like an inauspicious fruit
All black inside
By the time I understand what is truth
The life's journey is over
The road to travel is over.

What is this urge of mine
To put out a life burning so brightly
With spray of water!
Which burns
Burns with intention to convert to ashes
And in this small amount of ash
Whatever dreams peep out
Those are enough to fill life again
And inspire eternally to reach the inaccessible sky.

For that only this journey
The footsteps going ahead
Does not stop
With anyone's soothing words
The marks left of a burn injury
Does not disappear.
All have to go forward
And there would not be a point of return.

An Unknown Thrill

Many a time I have thought of
Uttering such a word
At whose effect
The seaward river shall stop on the halfway
Containing everything to itself
In the north moving wind
A delight of breeze shall be filled
The sky ward flying birds
And the whole universe shall be
Stupefied
The whole creation shall be disturbed
With an unknown delight.

I do not know how
In an intimate feeling
Words affect me
How the magic of the words

After the school bell rings
Go on their own
Without waiting
In their choicest direction.

What is in fact in it when the class is over
That is only a siren for break
And a call for sojourn in a plan of a long journey.

Sometimes I do not know;
Why a self-doubt
Compels us not to agree that it is a vacation.
All the known and unknown in this world
Relationships and tussles
All are resolved and levelled
By this long break of vacation.

In getting this leave
There is no willingness or unwillingness.
There is nothing even to keep aside
One's own beliefs
Only one has to wait for that
Special moment
Be it consciously or unconsciously.

A Journey

In a never-ending journey
At the start, I have to travel alone
In unknown and unseen paths.
How long you would carry your envy and ego
In the transparent glass pieces
And shall walk and walk on carrying a tired body.

So much of pain and feeling of loneliness
One cannot just see himself
And also cannot show off it to others,
Besides only a sympathetic expression.
But everything is in one's knowledge
Whatever on the other side
The falsity and temporariness
Still I hide in a shell of   deceit Inside me
And at last he arrives.

All my love, pang of separation, union
Dedication, sacrifice and insidious intent
Become meaningless in a moment.

Anything can leave a mark
The sudden bomb explosion
Or the mood of people who love to dream
for a million years.
Every breath of us appears
As if the whole world around is in fire
From time immemorial.
So many dreams have been burnt
And along with it so many dreams,
Attachments, memories
And even the symptoms of forbearance and sacrifices
Are devoured by fire.

Even for a moment I dedicate myself
To the call of a timepiece.
I get lost closing my eyes
With my hands raised
Before that unintelligible word.
But from my toe to head
Something, a thrilling experience mesmerizes me
And makes me speechless eternally.

The Bird

I have taken notice of
The bird since long.
I have counted the feathers of the bird
I have also found out how many are lost
And how many are left
I have assessed; how long it would fly
And when it would fall from the sky
Believe me, I have all these details.

The bird can chirp
And can create commotion
In a lonely and stunned silence.
It can create fear
By fluttering its wings in my heart
And can break it into pieces.
From there it can fly elsewhere also.
But I have kept all those records.

What is the necessity
To put the bird inside a cage !
What is the use to keep so many records
And again and again count the days
Till someone returns!!
Why I shall complain
Against all the strained relations!!

Who would ask about how I spent my life time?
In a moment I can break the sharp beak of the bird
I can cut off the flying wings.
I do not need to dream anymore.
No more I would measure my life
With profit and loss
I even do not need to leave this earth
With so much repentance and remorse.

Let the bird fly and fly
Until it becomes still by itself
I have all the accounts of the bird
Let it fly ceaselessly in a circle.

Fullstop

It would have been better
If I had put a stop there.
All these fake transactors
Crowd the market.
They do not even have a word with them
Not even they have a line of poem.
But they bargain
All the commodities in that market.

In front of them the girl in tattered clothes
Who in the guise of a beggar
Shows off her body
And all the eyes gather on her
With feigned sympathy.

I do not know when the sun sets
While I gather all the changes and coins

I have received it all day long.
By that time the customer disappears in darkness
And in his place a demon
Appears when I arrange the glass tumbler.

Oh! is he not the person who shouted shlogan
In the morning against poverty!
Is he the person who after bathing squeezed water from
The cloth he wore last night
And dried them on the torn petals of flowers!!

No!
It is not required to go ahead
And look for those dreamers
with uncontrolled emotions
In those lanes.
Rather it would have been better
Had I put a full stop there.

To Love

The moon had already undressed
The body of the night.
Some kind of inebriety
Was filled in youthfulness
To burn the hot summer days.
A fluid kiss of the moon
Was extinguishing the
Fire of the crowded world
At the time
All the inefficiencies of men
Were robbed of as if by the pirates in high seas
The impending moment's identity.

The dark night never
Differentiates between
Darkness and stigma attached with someone
All the slanders against me
Glow on the forehead of the night
like an ornament adorning my forehead.

My love has never been
A calculation on a mathematical formula
It also cannot turn into sometimes a moon
Sometimes a flower
Or a passionate kiss
Or it can be an uncontrolled wind.

From the flower of this earth
To the moon on the sky
Night wades from one end to the other
With the satisfaction of union.
Swimming across the vast seven seas
Sweet dreams come
And when at the daybreak
They all turn into murderers
And kill my emotions, attractions
And my aloneness.

After that ask myself.
Why these dreams come
And makes me spellbound.
That question puzzles me
And troubles me birth after birth
Remaining unsolved.
I do not know when
The answer shall be revealed to me
Regarding my love.

Reverberations

Each and every Moment
Is slipping away from my fist.
One aged body and mind
Appeared somehow transformed into
One sad and colourless form
Like a palm tree struck with thunder.
Like a man cut off from the society
I have been waiting for long
With vacant eyes
From one corner to the other corner of the earth.
Whatever I see are not mine
Whatever come to my thoughts are not my own
Whatever I get I cannot claim
Whatever I lose also I know was not mine.
At last, with an incompleteness
It dawns upon me that
The way I have come
I must depart in the same way.

I only could realise that
This earth has given me everything.
The flowers, the fruits, dreams, life and
The purpose to live, delight and passion
Everything granted by life.
As what one wishes to gather
He gets that only.
What more is then demanded for!!

But this is a different earth
In a narrow crevice an elephant can make way
But it's difficult for an ant to slip.
An ant's whole life is a run for food
And for an elephant for generations
He has stored immeasurable wealth.
Who would ask the details of it?
But nobody knows how from one's control
Time slips away.

Someone within five years
Someonewithin five days
Someone within five hours
Someone within five seconds
Can effect transmigration of soul
And change body
From a human body to take a monkey's body
If not a sheep's body
And start jumping from one branch to another.

The country is in danger!
The engagements and commitments of whole life
Get imprisoned in a tavern
And for that only everywhere

Wine shops are open.
But have you ever heard the throbs of life
And have you ever felt how life reverberates!
Life is for a moment
As if in a spell of dream
And uncontrolled whims.
If once it is lost
You have to wait for another life.

Completeness

Before you know about life
Life is over
And with it all the acquaintances
And relations are over.
Everywhere an indifference
Traps you in a spider's web
Making you melancholic
And you get lost every moment.

Can you tell anyone
Your so much pain and
How suffering makes one's life complete!
How can a person know
How an unseen force
Drags you from earth to the mythical cycle of time.
How does the sky exist
Getting totally unattached from me!
From my infatuation for life
And all my attractions and what I call my own!!

In this wide expanse of the space
I have come to know.
There is also purpose in flying
like a free dust particle.
Where do I reach
I am already there
When I search, who actually I am
I am also that entity.

Who says to me
To leave me on the halfway
Till I reach there!
There only in the spread of my own entity
I can visualise all the universe and the outer space,
The whole which is visible and invisible universe.
Everything mingles into me
To create a beautiful world.

A Kiss

Innumerable kisses
I have gathered from the whole world.
In an area where nobody has been able to reach
Those are stored.

Those all are not only memories
But are put as memorials of the lost time.
Sometimes all these things I lose and become worthless.

Sometimes all my own people
Become strangers
And I search them
Amidst all my engagements.
Behind those efforts of mine
Somewhere a trace of woe
Almost of a needle point measure
Is hidden.
Those overpower me
And make me helpless and immobile
For all times to come.

Now a kiss is
Even more deadly than an atom bomb
And prepares itself to put the whole universe
Into flames.

This is even more dreadful than
Any infectious disease.
I just spread and minutely examined
several worm-eaten and decayed Kisses
inside me
which looked like an untidy overgrowth of plants and dirt.
Somewhere I saw my father
And in some places my mother's face appeared
In some other places my near dears
And close relations.
All of them had become chapters of history
And were like the archeological remains
The bone of Buddha
Asking for investigations and great research.

Now all these kisses reserved
Are for a conjugal relationship
And for youthful love between a boy and girl.
Oh! What a feeling of sweetness and intoxication !
Everywhere it seemed
As if one fortification of intimate relationship
And feeling of appreciation
Crumbles.
Yes, everything was over
Another demon had already started
his wayward exploitation.

Deceit

Nobody dared to touch it
The people who talked of their
Bravery and daredevilry
Almost bowed before
What is truth
Have been loss of words.

Someone told.
Yes, yes, If not so with Asharam
We are very close to Nityanand.
We live with lies
We write lies
Even we have constructed such a world
Where it's impossible to climb the steps of Truth.

I not only listened to them
I was in the audience.
It was a golden opportunity

To meet the carriers of a tradition.
I was not able to see my faults
And follies
Whatever defects I saw
Those were in others,
Alas!!

From sunrise till the sun sets
From a daybreak to time when a day passes
Months after months
And years after years
Ever after a million of ages
The sky, the atmosphere
And the planets and satellites
The zodiacs and the stars
Might change.
But one voice
Reverberates in my ear,
How with self-deceit
I have been acting beautifully
And how others deceive others
By demonstrating, how they are impressed
With me.

Lost Childhood

I feel something is lost from me
Since long.
The sensations full of dreams
Are spreading all over my nerves.
Inside me there is incessant rain
And the ravages of untimely storm
And a purposeless silent uncontrolled leap,
My mind spreads all over.

Sometimes in me a sky full of stars is drawn
And miles after miles of wish flowers
Bloom in abundance.
Sometimes a desolate sky
Shows me myriads of dreams.

The long highway which connects
Our village with the town
Appears strange and unknown
In my thoughts.

The mirage visible in the cruel sun
Was asking me about the green paddy fields,
Chirping of birds, southern wind
and a foggy winter.

No,
All these were lost long before
In the maelstrom of time.
Now days I face a peculiar loneliness
Overpowering me.
There was no sensation when someone touched me
Also, I was not eager to know about it.
All these merged and have reached
A peak beyond my reach.

How many more days

I do not know
How many more days!

I got a body
A mind
An emotion
But out of these which shall I take with me!!

Whatever I call mine
Are they mine!
You have given me a moonlit sky
Innumerable dreams
You have given me also
Pounds of flesh.
But I do not know why I am afraid to tell you
That you are mine only.

Can I show it to others
The mind with orientation for you !
I see every day
my exact image there
But I wonder, how you kept it
So transparent and clear.

Tell me what else I would have given you:
I have given words
And a beautiful structure built of words
I have given you my poems
To perceive me as per your wish
For many more births to come.
Still, I find myself
Strange and unknown to me
Being unaware of it
That I am shedding tears
And go on thinking.

What you know of me
That is still unknown to me.
A question permanently peeps
From me;
Who am I.
Do you know really
Who am I??

All the time I feel
How could you make me
Giving me so many thoughts and emotions!
The whole sky looks so small

In you
How all the words lose meanings
With the gush of your breath!!

Are you afraid as
No one can restrict you within words!
No one can keep you inside his tears
Which you apprehend.
Still, you revolve round me
As an invisible entity.
Sometimes you touch me
And disappear at the next moment
Ask myself, how many more days
This would be!!

Births after births
I shall be searching you in
Heaven, earth and abyss.
Wherever you be
You would be in the lookout for me.
In this eternal search the heavenly delight
I shall have
Let it be permanently with me.

The Last word: Hope

Hope is a flying bird
Can the calling of that bird
Ever be over!!
No one can stop the movement
Of that flying bird.

As because that bird flies
We see dreams on this earth
And build boats
To sail across the sea of the World.

When everything is inundated by darkness
A feeble ray of light
Encourages us to live.
It becomes the company of the lonely man
And reaches us in a new world
Painting it with the colour of poetry.

Whenever adversity comes
We pray that invisible power with folded hands.
Can anybody ascertain
When our life would without purpose
And it would be purposeful !!

It's only a glimmer of hope
Which draws you to yourself
Consoles us to face every accident and incidents
In our life.

BLACK EAGLE BOOKS

www.blackeaglebooks.org
info@blackeaglebooks.org

Black Eagle Books, an independent publisher, was founded as a nonprofit organization in April, 2019. It is our mission to connect and engage the Indian diaspora and the world at large with the best of works of world literature published on a collaborative platform, with special emphasis on foregrounding Contemporary Classics and New Writing.

www.ingramcontent.com/pod-product-compliance
Lightning Source LLC
Chambersburg PA
CBHW060619080526
44585CB00013B/903